ST. PATRICK'S DAY

A Crowell Holiday Book

ST. PATRICK'S DAY

BY
MARY CANTWELL

Illustrated by Ursula Arndt

Thomas Y. Crowell Company New York

CROWELL HOLIDAY BOOKS

Edited by Susan Bartlett Weber

NEW YEAR'S DAY	LABOR DAY
LINCOLN'S BIRTHDAY	THE JEWISH NEW YEAR
ST. VALENTINE'S DAY	COLUMBUS DAY
WASHINGTON'S BIRTHDAY	UNITED NATIONS DAY
PURIM	HALLOWEEN
ST. PATRICK'S DAY	ELECTION DAY
PASSOVER	THANKSGIVING DAY
ARBOR DAY	HUMAN RIGHTS DAY
MAY DAY	HANUKKAH
MOTHER'S DAY	CHRISTMAS
FLAG DAY	THE JEWISH SABBATH
THE FOURTH OF JULY	SKIP AROUND THE YEAR

ST. PATRICK'S DAY

Every March, for many years, a parade line was painted down the middle of Fifth Avenue in New York City. Most street lines are white or yellow, but this one was bright green. It was a tribute to St. Patrick, the patron saint of Ireland. The green line is no longer painted, but St. Patrick is still honored with a parade every year.

Because millions of Americans have Irish ancestors, Patrick is a much-loved saint in the United States. He died more than fifteen hundred years ago, on March 17. Each year, on this day, many American cities have a parade. New York's is the biggest.

Bands playing Irish songs march along Fifth Avenue. Drums beat. The flags of the Republic of Ireland and the United States flutter in the crisp spring air. Children carry their school banners. Men sell green-and-gold pennants and big, bright balloons to the children who are watching.

On this day, Irishmen all over the world wear something green. They put green carnations in their buttonholes. They pin little sprigs of shamrock, a small green plant that looks like clover, on their coats. Or they may wear green neckties.

Most people think the Irish wear green on St. Patrick's Day because Ireland is called the Emerald Isle. The real reason is almost forgotten now. Hundreds of years ago, in Ireland, the people burned green leaves and boughs in the spring. Then they spread the ashes over the fields, believing this would make the land richer. The man who wears something green is honoring that ancient custom, even though he may not know it.

On St. Patrick's Day, many people go to church. They give thanks to God for sending St. Patrick to Ireland.

Patrick died in Ireland, but he was born in England, probably in 385. No one knows exactly when or where. His family were Christians. His father, Calpurnius, was a deacon in the Christian church. Patrick's grandfather, Potitius, was a Christian priest.

At that time, England was a part of the Roman Empire. So was most of Europe. The great Roman army had fought and won great battles in many countries. Roman soldiers settled in the lands they had conquered and taught the people their Roman ways.

Before the Romans came to England, the English lived in tribes, hunting, fishing, weaving, and bee-keeping. Often their houses were made of mud. There were no real towns.

The Romans changed everything. They taught the English how to read and write in Latin. They built wonderful roads. You can still ride on some of them today, although they are more than fifteen hundred years old.

The Romans had mail deliveries. They knew
how to heat houses. They even knew about hot
and cold running water.

They built cities and surrounded them with
walls. Parts of the Roman walls still stand in
England today. One famous part is in the base-
ment of the Bank of England, in London.

But slowly the Roman Empire was crushed by tribes of wild men, called barbarians. Most of them came from northern Europe.

They did not come to build cities, like the Romans. They came to rob and destroy. Because they burned schools and libraries, many people never learned to read and write. The Roman soldiers had to return to Europe, and fight for Rome.

The English had no army of their own. When the Romans went, there was no one left to protect them.

One day, when Patrick was about sixteen years old, a band of Irish pirates swept down upon the English coast. They came in brown-sailed boats, blowing their bronze war trumpets.

The pirates burned and looted houses, and captured one thousand Englishmen. Patrick was one of them. He was taken across the Western Sea—we call it the Irish Sea—to Ireland, and sold into slavery.

Patrick became a shepherd. Although no one knows for sure, we think his master was a tribal chieftain named Miliucc. Miliucc lived near the great hill of Slemish, in the north of Ireland.

At that time, there were very few Christians in Ireland. Most Irishmen worshipped the sun and moon and stars.

Their teachers were called Druids. The Druids had great power over the people because it was believed they could foretell the future. The Irish thought the Druids understood all the mysteries of the world.

Patrick was lonely and frightened in Ireland. For six years, he prayed for help. He wrote, "I used to get up for prayer before daylight, through snow, through frost, through rain. . . ."

One night, while Patrick lay sleeping in the fields with his sheep, he heard a voice. It said, "Soon you will go to your own country."

Later, he heard the voice again. This time it said, "See, your ship is ready."

So Patrick escaped his master. Alone, he fled through the countryside.

At that time, Ireland was covered with trees. Traveling was difficult and dangerous. Many of the Irish tribesmen who lived in the forests were savage, and cruel to strangers.

But Patrick was unharmed. Finally, after a hard journey, he arrived at a seaport. There he found a boat made of skins, with sails of linen, making ready to leave Ireland. Sailors were loading the boat with Irish wolfhounds, tall, lean hunting dogs with tails like plumes.

The boat, with its cargo of dogs, was going to Gaul, which is now called France. At first, the sailors did not want to take Patrick, but after he begged them, they agreed.

After a three-day voyage, the boat arrived in Gaul. The country was a wilderness. It had been invaded by fierce tribes who had ruined the land.

Patrick and the sailors walked for twenty-eight days in search of a town and people. They had no food, and were weak and faint from hunger. No one knows what happened to the wolf-hounds. Perhaps they journeyed through Gaul with the sailors.

One day, a herd of pigs suddenly appeared on the road before them. Running as fast as they could, the sailors chased them across the empty land. At last, some were captured, killed, and roasted for dinner.

Very tired, but no longer hungry, the sailors and Patrick rested for two days. Then they walked on again. They wandered for ten days, until they found a village where people still lived.

Now Patrick and the sailors parted. No one is sure where Patrick went. Some people believe he journeyed to the monastery at Lérins, an island off the coast of southern France.

At that time, monasteries were something like the colleges of today. Brilliant men lived, studied, and taught in them.

Patrick stayed several years in Gaul. Then he went home to England.

Patrick's family was very happy to see him. But soon after Patrick arrived, he had a strange dream. In this dream, a man called Victoricus came to him from Ireland. Victoricus carried a letter which said, "The voice of the Irish . . . asks thee, boy, come and walk with us once more."

Patrick believed that God was telling him to bring his Christian faith to the people of Ireland. He had to obey. So Patrick left his home and family once again.

Before going back to Ireland, Patrick returned to Gaul. He studied at Auxerre, another monastery, for a long time. He wanted to learn everything he could about the Christian faith.

When Patrick finished his studies, a bishop named Germanus made him a priest. Then Patrick left for Ireland. This time, however, he was no longer a shepherd and a slave. He was, instead, a Christian bishop.

Patrick took with him gold and silver orna-
ments for the churches he would build. He also
had needlewomen to make the priests' robes and
hangings for the altars. There were assistants to
help Patrick spread the words of Christ. And
there were charioteers to carry Patrick and his
priests throughout Ireland.

One of the few Irish Christians, a chieftain named Dichu, gave Patrick a wooden barn. It became his first church. From there, Patrick traveled through Ireland, telling people of Christ's life and miracles.

He baptized the people in the country's streams and wells. Some of these are still called "St. Patrick's wells."

During those years, Patrick was often nearly captured by savage tribes. There were many plots against his life. But he let nothing stop him from teaching Christianity.

At first, the Druids were Patrick's enemies. They feared he would take away their power. But when they heard Patrick talk of Christ, many became Christians. Some even became priests.

Patrick became famous in Ireland, and many tales of his magic were told. They are like fairy tales, and most of them are not true.

One well-known story says that Patrick drove the snakes from Ireland. In another, Patrick has a wrestling match with a devil and wins.

Still other stories say that Patrick escaped capture by an enemy by turning himself and his followers into a herd of deer. And that when a Druid wizard put poison into Patrick's drink, Patrick turned it into ice and tossed it from his cup. Another legend tells how a friend of Patrick's was protected from a fire because he was wearing Patrick's cloak.

These tales are exciting, but it is the truth about Patrick that makes him great. He saved the Romans' learning for the world.

The Druids had their own alphabet, called ogam. They kept it a secret among themselves, refusing to share it with anyone. This meant that no one but the Druids could read.

But Patrick and his priests taught the Latin alphabet to everyone they baptized. This was very important. Many years later, when all Europe had been conquered by savage tribes, the Irish could still read and write in Latin.

They still had libraries and schools. They were able to keep and pass on to their children all the knowledge of the Romans.

Little more is known of Patrick's life. Some say he left Ireland again and went to Rome. There he may have seen the Pope, who was head of the Christian church.

We do know that Patrick wrote a small book about his adventures. It is called *Confessio*, which means "Confession." One can still see ancient copies of it in a few great libraries. The original, in Patrick's own handwriting, disappeared more than a thousand years ago. He also founded a large church and monastery in Armagh, a part of Ireland.

We know, too, that Patrick died in 461. But we do not know where he was buried. There is no splendid tomb of St. Patrick. He is simply a part of the Irish soil.

But because of him, Ireland kept the light of learning alive when the rest of the world was dark. That is why, on every March 17, men march, drums beat, and flags fly for St. Patrick.

ABOUT THE AUTHOR

Mary Cantwell grew up in Bristol, Rhode Island, and is a graduate of Connecticut College. She has written for *Vogue, Vogue Children,* and *Mademoiselle,* and she is now the chief copywriter for *Mademoiselle.*

Mary Cantwell lives with her husband and two daughters in New York City.

ABOUT THE ILLUSTRATOR

Ursula Arndt always liked to draw the things she saw and read about and decided to become an illustrator at a very early age.

Besides illustrating children's books, she has designed a delightful series of Christmas cards.

Ursula Arndt grew up in Düsseldorf, West Germany, where she attended the Academy of Arts and took special studies in etching. She has traveled in France, Holland, Italy, and Yugoslavia. She now lives in New York City.